# LOVE *in* OLD AGE

# LOVE *in* OLD AGE

*And other plain-written poems.*
*All written with poetic discipline.*
*All easily understandable.*
*And even some that rhyme.*

TONY ANTIN

Mill City Press, Inc.
322 First Avenue N, 5th floor
Minneapolis, MN 55401
612.455.2293
www.millcitypublishing.com



ISBN-13: 978-1-63413-499-6
LCCN: 2015906298

**Production/Composition by Parker Antin**
**Illustrations by Robert Mesrop**

*Printed in the United States of America*

*For Jean—*

*and for the loving last of life*

*we share.*

## PRAISE FOR TONY ANTIN'S PLAIN-WRITTEN POEMS

". . . straightforward . . . clean and delightful to read."

—*Reader Views*

". . . an amazing set of poems. Full of happiness, sadness, love, humor and wisdom . . ."

—*Readers' Favorite*

". . . down-to-earth poet pulls your eyes smoothly down the page, getting meaning from every word . . . "

—*Beth's Book Review Blog*

". . . sings with evocative imagery and wonderfully satisfying form."

—Kathleen Henderson Staudt, PhD, author of *Civilization: David Jones and Modern Poetics*

". . . disciplined, delightful dance of words."

—*Richard Legrand*

". . . highly recommended for all who love poetry."

—*Midwest Book Review*

". . . treasure disguised as plain-written poems."

—*Ronald Sirch*

". . . simply touched my heart."

—*Dr. Clare Zhang*

# Contents

# Introduction

I DOUBT I'M ALONE in being at serious odds with what's accepted and published as poetry these days. It seems that all you need to do to make a poem is write something, break it up into short lines, and set them in stanzas. (Three lines seem to be the current choice.) No need to worry about how the lines and stanzas break or whether the breaks make a bit of sense. Just make the whole thing *look* like a poem on the page. *Poems by typography!*

Worse, much, much worse: No concern about anyone else understanding what you have written. In fact, it seems accepted that the deeper the ambiguity, the more prestigious the poem. Take, for example, poems in the *New Yorker* and, of all places, in *Poetry* magazine. I've heard it said in a poetry group, "Poetry is a very personal thing. If it has meaning to the poet, that's all that counts." Then why publish it? Put it in your diary!

Poetry is to the art of writing what ballet is to the art of dance. Poetry differs from prose in that a poet attempts (or should attempt) to express or communicate not only with word meanings but also (and critically so) within word schemes. Word patterns. Flows of rhythm. Schemes, patterns, and rhythms that add to the power, the meaning, the effect of the words; the ease of reading them. But which—and this is what so many of the published poems ignore today—also *set up boundaries within which the poet must work.*

Long ago, that meant rhythm and rhyme. For some of us, for *some* poems, it still does, when what we are trying to say or express comes off best that way. Even when it's appropriate to work in free verse, I adhere to the boundaries I set up for each poem. That's the challenge. That's what makes poetry entirely different from prose.

I hold Robert Frost above all poets. Best for unique insights, for humanity, emotion, for story, and for technique. In his first published book, *A Boy's Will*, filled with poems of love and nature, are masterpieces of rhythm *and* rhyme. But his next book, *North of Boston*, would be filled with episodes of New Englanders speaking. To have these people talk in rhyme would, of course, be ludicrous. So he turned here to a scheme without rhyme. Ah, but still totally a scheme. A word plan, with boundaries within which he wrote.

Open to any one of those poems and count the syllables. Always ten, and always with rhythm. Every one of those so natural sounding; conversation and narration within a predetermined word pattern. (Here and there, those Frost lines might count nine or eleven syllables, but they all *read* like ten.) To Frost, totally undisciplined free verse was, in his words, "playing tennis with the net down." To that I add, and with no boundary chalk lines, either.

There is, of course, a place for free verse. When that is the appropriate form for the poem. A number of the poems in this book are free (or semi-free) verse. But . . . *but* . . . to be poetry, free verse must exhibit artistic discipline (emphasis on *artistic* and *discipline*). There must be poetic reason for what the poet does. Lines must be broken and words placed to pull your eyes smoothly down through the poem. And leave you, at the end, saying, *"Yes!"*

Tony Antin, 2015

## Love in Old Age

*"Grow old along with me!*
*The best is yet to be,*
*the last of life, for which the first was made."*
*Robert Browning*

If they had asked me then
if I remembered when
I first realized that I was deep in love with you,

I would have said, I knew
when first I kissed with you
and felt the love, the warmth flow through your lips
to mine.

And then through all the years
of happiness and tears
the love I felt was always there and seemed
unchanged.

But now in our old age
we've turned another page,
and in this last of life I've learned a sweeter love.

It's nothing like before.
It's something so much more.
A deep and loving kinship's part of what's there now.

*continued*

And seeing in your face
through lines that aging trace,
    the soft and gentle beauty I have always loved.

And I, at last, have learned
what I had not discerned:
    that you will always keep a private part of you.

The best, the best of all
decisions I recall
    the best I've made was asking you to marry me.

*(To be added after I am gone.)*
And now that I have closed
my eyes in last repose,
    I chose, I hope, the kindest time to say good-bye.

## Verse Too Free

Think of the sport of competitive dancing:
You have to perform the steps of the dance.
Then you can add in the art of enhancing
to give your performance a prize-winning chance.

Now think of the poems of a long-ago day:
You had to conform to a rhythm with rhyme.
Then you would add (if you could) to your say
artistic touches to make the bells chime.

Note, in both cases, the two separate parts.
First showing perfection in what is *required*.
Then *adding* the sine qua non of the arts:
thrilling revealing of brilliance inspired.

Think now of what we call poems today:
There's no demonstration of mastering a form.
No rhythm, no rhyme, no rules to obey.
Free verse we call it, and that's now the norm.

But letting the run-of-the-mill wannabe
claim it's a poem when what's written shows
only lazy dependence upon the word "free"
is simply accepting more broken line prose.

## The Tide Comes Back

Have you ever seen a river
    that's been frozen clear across
    with tide gone out from underneath the ice?
When something that was whole
    now lay in broken slabs,
    some pieces flat on mud,
    some tilted up by stubs of reeds
    left over from last fall,
    and even some
    pushed partway onto others?
What once was strong and solid
now broken
as though defeated.

I've despaired through times
when life seemed much the same,
    the pieces all apart,
    with what supported them before
gone out from underneath.

In such spirit-empty times,
    what's kept my hope from going slack
    was knowing that the tide comes back.

## Heart Failure

*Written on a hospital bed, when first told diagnosis.*

At last (and at least)
I have learned
what will end my life.

And I'm disappointed.

I had thought it might be
something more traumatic
something more climactic.
I had *hoped* it would be
something clean and neat
that I could calmly meet
with cool indifference.

Like all men,
        I would rather drop than sink.
        I don't want all that time to think.

## Ruefully

Ruefully,
I smile at the time
when I felt no danger.
The days when death
was a distant stranger.
Now after years
of love and labor,
ruefully,
I smile at my new
and awaiting neighbor.

## Deathbed Embarrassment

*(If I have a deathbed.)*

I'm afraid I'll be embarrassed
on the day that I die.
I'm just so damned emotional
I'm afraid that I'll cry.

## Hello, Mr. Death

Hello, Mr. Death.
(Or is it Mrs. . . . or, possibly, Miss?)
Whichever the gender,
come, give me your bittersweet
kiss.

## Confession of a Plain-Writing Poet

I simply cannot poem
a line that has no meaning
to others who will read it
with rightful expectation
that they will understand me.

If what I want to do is
communicate a message,
I feel an obligation
to so compose to make it
clear to those who read my words.

Or if I want to share some
enchanting scene of nature,
I've got to write the vision

*continued*

so that they, too, will see it . . .
the loveliness I savored.

Or if I have an insight
that might perhaps enlighten
some subtle part of living,
I should not leave my readers
in the dark on what I mean.

You may, perhaps, have noticed
I've made these lines adhere to
a predetermined pattern
of syllables and rhythm.
That's what makes an essay
a poem.

## To Spite the Thing

When I just can't remember a word,
in revolt against this aging blight
I blurt out whatever words will come.
(And do it with a wonderful feeling of spite!)
So what if I want but can't call up "macaroni."
Revenge is mine when I spit out, "Caledonia!"
Last night, my equally aging wife,
had intended to bake brownies for the fair.
But one thing after another
(including a couple of nod-off naps)
stole away the evening hours.
In the bedroom as we turned the covers down,
I noted: "You never got to bake . . .
                                        the . . . *egg foo yung*!"
She knew exactly what I meant!

## A Crew Blessing

*In an eight-man crew, the* **coxswain** *steers and jockeys the race, the* **stroke** *must be the first to "find and give more,"* **seven** *must precisely take the cadence from stroke,* **six** *to* **three** *are the mid-shell muscle of the boat, and the* **bow two** *are the first to feel and handle rough water.*

May
you have
the smarts of a cox,
the guts of a stroke,
the empathy of a seven,
the strength of a mid-shell,
and the hands of the bow two.

## Why a Poem?

A poem is a poet's urge
to say something.
But not simply to *tell* it
as truly to *reveal* it.
And if, once so revealed,
it makes some reader say,
"Yes! I see! That's right!
And so rightly written!"
then the poem goes
beyond the *urge*
to the deepest *hope*
of the poet.

## Sculler's Winter

While I slept, the cold confined my lake.

Only yesterday,
my boats de-rigged and covered,
I had stood shore-bound
remembering how the autumn sunlight
made a rippling, sparkling surface
through which my shell's bow sliced,
in which my oars
            left swirling puddles,
on which the fallen yellow leaves
swept by as I
with joy rowed through them.
Both of us alive,
the lake and I.

But while I slept, a sheet of silver ice
as much as buried all the water.
And left, it seems to me, a frozen shroud.

## Sculler's Code

I've tried to row through life
and hope to take my final strokes
sitting tall.
Left hand over right,
holding perfect form.
Always doing it right,
or not at all.

## Soliloquy for a Football Coach

To kick or not to kick: That is the question.
Whether 'tis nobler in the mind to harvest
The single point that kicking's always offered,
Or to try to pass or rush through yon opponent,
And, by succeeding, *beat* them. To win; to tie
No more; and by that win to say we end
The heartache and the thousand natural shocks
Coaches are heir to, 'tis a consummation
Devoutly to be wished. To win, to try;
To try; perchance to *lose*; ay, there's the rub;
For in to stop the play what foes may come
When we have started out to run or pass,
Must give us pause. There's the respect
That makes calamity of so long odds.
For who would bear the whips and scorns of scribes,
Commentators' wrongs, the owner's contumely,
The fangs of angry fans, career's delay,
The insolence of players and the spurns
Of good-bye chants from stadium stands,
When he himself might a safe tying take
With a sure placekick? Who would take the dare
To pass o'er or plow into a mulish line,
And bear the dread of being stopped just short

Of that rewarding country from whose bourn
No points are easy earned? This softens will,
And makes us rather take one point we can
Than try for two so far from sure.
Thus caution does make cowards of us all;
And thus the native hue of resolution
Is sicklied o'er with the pale cast of doubt.
And so I shall not try to pass or run it.
With this resolve, we'll kick it, and at least
Not lose this game of action. Soft you now!
The ball is snapped! Gods, in thy heavens,
Be my good deeds remembered.

## Alone in Death

"It was nice," we like to say.
"He died peacefully in his sleep, you know.
    When my time comes,
    that's how I want to go."

But I can't let that stand as right.
I'll bet
it snapped his eyelids open in the night,
that sudden, certain knowledge
the dying surely get.
Perhaps he even tried
but couldn't lift his arm—
to wake the sleeping form beside him
as he perspired his alarm;
wanting, trying, struggling to call
*"Please . . . somebody . . . please!"*
I just can't see a silent turning to the wall,
not wanting to disturb the family's ease.

That's what we won't face up to,
the fact he *might* have suffered deep
during our own pleasant sleep.

I think we shunt a guilt to say,
"He felt no pain."
And pretend he simply sighed away
a final breath.
I think because we know
we could as well have said,
"We were not there for him.
He was alone in death."

## Tired of Me

I've lived with me a long, long time.
  I'm not too far from ninety-three
And lately I've been noticing
  that I sometimes get tired of me.

I can't say *bored*, that's not the word.
  It's much more like, "Oh yeah, so what?"
And life's quite good, that's not to blame.
  And I'm content with what I've got.

But same old thoughts and same old things,
  and same old, same old points of view,
They're just as good, they're just as bad.
  But also, "So, what else is new?"

So even if I don't agree
  with what you say and what you do,
  may I, please, sometimes be you?

## Slow This Engine Down

*An audience-participation poem/song, sung to the tune of "Wabash Cannonball." Audience joins in on the chorus.*

*(Chorus)*

My engine's always racing,
redline every day.
Running overheated,
can't go on this way.
Always feeling tired,
never sleeping sound.
Where's the carburetor
to slow this engine down?

Down, down, down.
teedle-ee-dee,
down, down, down.

*(Verse)*

They said to give up coffee,
and brew some herbal tea.
Then sit and sip and sip and sit
as quiet as I can be.
I tried it with some chamomile
and other herbals, too.
None of them were any good,
they took *too long* to brew.

*continued*

Brew, brew, brew.
teedle-ee-dee,
brew, brew, brew.

*(Chorus - Sing Along)*
Sooo, my engine is still racing,
redline every day.
Running overheated,
can't go on this way.
Always feeling tired,
never sleeping sound.
Where's the carburetor
to slow this engine down?

Down, down, down,
teedle-ee-dee,
down, down, down.

*(Verse)*
Someone suggested fishing
with nothing on for bait.
And then to sit there patiently,
and wait and wait and wait.
I did as was suggested,
and thought I did it right.
But I was interrupted
every time I felt a bite.

Bite, bite, bite,
teedle-ee-dee
bite, bite, bite.

*(Chorus - Sing Along)*
Sooo, my engine is still racing,
redline every day.
Running overheated,
can't go on this way.
Always feeling tired,
never sleeping sound.
Where's the carburetor,
to slow this engine down?

Down, down, down.
teedle-ee-dee,
down, down, down.

*(Verse)*
I tried some meditation,
sitting all alone.
Fingertips together,
disconnected phone.
I listened to my breathing,
and softly hummed a song.
Had to give that up because
the sessions took *too long*.

*continued*

Long, long, long,
teedle-ee-dee,
long, long, long.

*(Chorus - Sing Along)*
Sooo, my engine is still racing,
redline every day.
Running overheated,
can't go on this way.
Always feeling tired,
never sleeping sound.
Where IS the carburetor
to s-l-o-w . . .
t-h-i-s . . .
e-n-g-i-n-e . . .
d-o-w-n.

Teedle-ee-dee.
DOWN!

## No!

We view it as admirable sentimentality
                                        and deepest patriotism
to weep with loving, smiling faces,
to give our thanks
as we look out over the uniformed lines of crosses
beneath which lie the decomposing bodies
                                    of our once beautiful sons
                                                            and brothers and sisters
                                                            and neighborhood kids
                                                            and so many unknown.
We can't hear it, but from the ground
                                          thousands of voices
                                          murmur bitterly,
                                                            "No!"

"I did not volunteer to give my life.
I did not even want to *be* there.
        But I was forced into going.
Forced by the way the river of society flows.
Forced by the rules of what everyone expects
        of a good man . . . or a good woman.
        I was good.
        What was I to do?"
When they draped the flag over me,
        precisely folded and handed to them,
        when they shot rifles and played taps,

*continued*

all that while I was protesting,
"No! No! I want to be among *you*,
not here."

If we could hear their voices,
if we could put a cold light of reality
on our glorious annual
patriotic gratefulness
maybe . . . just maybe
we could change the direction
in which the river flows.
And stunt . . . even end
the ever-growing
fields of crosses.

## Rowing Rhymes

The stroke was high,
the crew was low.
Still, coxie upped the clip.
'till, one by one, from bow to stern,
the crew deserted ship.

*Competing crews used to bet their racing jerseys, leaving the losing crews bare-chested.*

The boys on the shore
gave forth with hurrahs
when they heard that the girls
had agreed to bet bras.

*As crews line up, "stake boat boys and girls" hold the shell sterns steady.*

The crew pulled strongly from the line,
but promptly fell three lengths behind.
They felt they had a whale in tow;
the stake boat boy had not let go.

## Humanism

Nobody knows and nobody cares
what frightens me. But that's all right.
"God" didn't put us here in pairs,
and promise to hold our hands at night.
(And, as a matter of fact, I used
the name of "God" poetically.)
However life on earth was fused,
no Father did it biblically.

Nobody knows and nobody cares
what frightens you. But it's all right
if nobody holds your hand and shares
the personal burden of your fright.
(And, as a matter of fact, I wish
this truth were known to everyone:
There's nobody there to catch your fish.
We weren't saved by any Son.)

Nobody knows and nobody cares
what frightens us. And that's all right.
Everyone's bearing what everyone bears.
And we all see what's in everyone's sight.
(And, as a matter of fact, I say
the day we know we *are* alone,
and no One is there to show the way,
we just might make it on our own.)

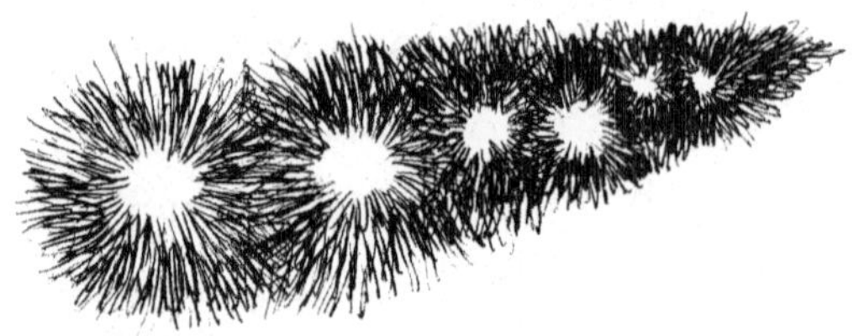

## Driving in My Nineties

Each set of headlights
that appears
and approaches
faster and faster
on the two-lane road
brings low-keyed anxiety
until it Dopplers by
just two feet away
from what I really don't expect
. . . and yet.

In my *eighteenth* year,
with nothing in my experience
to diminish
my own fresh freedom
at the wheel,
cars passed by
seen but not feared.

Certainly un-flinched,
sometimes admired,
and most likely embraced
as friends of the open road.

Now, in the years of my *nineties*,
I drive in a land of licensed lunatics.
Who *are* all these people,
and where in hell
are they all going?
It's snowing
and the idiots don't slow down.
I can't see around
that goddamned SUV.
And the asshole behind me
is way too close!

## Lonely Rooster

The lonely silver rooster,
arrow through its toes,
wavers in the wind
to show which way it blows.

Down beneath the steeple
people meet to pray,
hoping for directions
to find the peaceful way.

## Sport Shorts

The team deserved the whistle
for illegal use of hands.
And no one knew it better
than the coeds in the stands.

My golfing fault's no mystery.
I know what's wrong, doggone it.
My eye is always on the ball.
The club is what's not on it.

The goalie's mouth was open wide,
the puck went flying in.
At which some wag remarked, "The team
that gets a head will win."

She could not cut a figure eight,
but in her form-fit tights,
the figure that she did cut
scored a 10 for lovely sights.

## More Sport Shorts

The fans, they go wild,
the field, it goes deep,
when I go to bat
after going to sleep.

The crowd was praying for the time
to score once more and win!
The sponsors prayed for time to get
one more commercial in.

Tennis, they say, is a passionate game,
one for a villain and hero.
But I can't attach very deep feeling to
a game in which "love" is a zero.

The loud-mouthed bowler was all puffed up.
"I'm headed," he bragged, "for a perfect game."
But before he could sip from the victory cup,
he blew it in the top of the second frame.

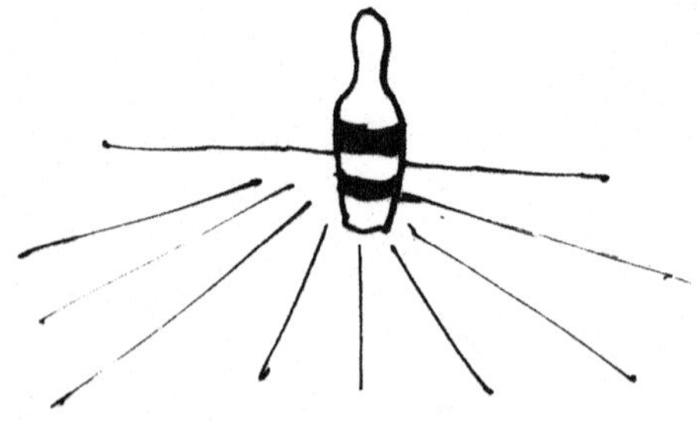

## David's Dead

The unthinking acceptance
    of our own immortality
is shaken
    by the passing of a peer.
Suddenly, we are in the game,
contestants now,
    playing by the year,
and wondering
    if we'll be the next
    about whom they ask,
"Oh, did you hear?"

## Loving Despair!

*Anguish of an atheist with dear and deeply religious friends.*

Oh, you who proclaim
  a supernatural being,
  you thrust me, bind me
  into anguished despair.
How can you claim a mind of reason
  when you assume it sane
  to say your god tells you
  of heaven for your holiness,
but cry insanity
  when others say
  their god tells them
  of paradise and virgins
  if they explode themselves
  while killing you?

Can't you see
  that by your acceptance
  of "thy will be done,"
you make legitimate
  the "will be done"
  of murderers?

Have you not noticed
    that your god has never stopped a war?
Do you not know
    how unyielding faiths
            have ignited
    and intensified so many?
And not only wars:
    god-condoned cruelties
    so horrible and merciless
    from racks to burning stakes,
    crusades and genocide!

I curse the cowardly,
            infantile expectation
of a mystic-guided road
            to a world of peace.
A world so tragically denied
by the obstructions
of your invented god.

## Did He Know I Cared?

*The hope of an ambulance crew chief.*

The radio dispatcher's calm voice had said,
"Ambulance needed at (giving an address).
No lights or siren,
you've been there before."

We had: A chronic case.
A "transport," almost scheduled
from home to hospital
back . . . and back.

And so, my taking pulse and pressure,
holding blue-veined wrist
and counting,
that was just routine,
a part of which
was glancing up
to check his color.

But this time, as I did
he sighed
and laid his head back
on the couch-converted bed,
so that instead of the usual
averted eyes,

I found his looking into mine.
Only this time his eyes said,
"Hell, I'm going to die."

And mine,
        I so hope he saw I cared
        when mine admitted,
                        "Yes . . .
                         Yes, I know."

## Nap Time

When may you, in public, take a nap
of, say, ten minutes, maybe more?
When, in a meeting, someone says,
"Let me repeat what I said before."

Or you can take a longer snooze,
with mind in neutral, far away
when through the fog you hear the words,
"And so, in brief, just let me say . . ."

And, in your sleep, if you should hear
six *other* words, you'll know they bring
a lot more time to stay passed out.
These six: "Oh, yes, just one more thing."

## The Blind Title

*Magazine editors sometimes put cleverness before clarity and write what they call "blind titles." They do this believing that readers will be attracted/intrigued by, say, a clever alliteration or play on words that otherwise gives no idea of what the article offers.*

The title was a blind one,
and the reader passed it by.
The editor was shocked
and demanded to know why.

"Oh, I don't know," the reader said,
"I guess it was because
I didn't catch a word upon
the page to make me pause."

"Well, damn it," said the editor,
"you ought to know that we,
the *pros* in editorial,
we have our needs to be
poetic and dramatic,
and blind titles fill that need.
It's *prosaic* to just give away
the reason you should read.
Why, *any*one at all
can write a title that reveals.

*continued*

True artistry is what it takes
to write one that conceals."

The reader sighed and said, "Well, yes
but every single day,
so many, many things I see
compete for me to stay.
I must admit," the reader said,
"and you, the pro, should know
that I will stop just where I see
the clearest quid pro quo."

The editor, now in despair,
with forehead in a hand,
bemoaned, "There's no use going on,
you just don't understand."
With that, the reader brightened
and with great relief said, "Well, you
finally got it right, 'cause that's
what I've been trying to tell you."

## Where an Atheist Goes to Church

*I'm a very comfortable member of the historic*
*Unitarian Church of Barnstable on Cape Cod.*

Where I go to church, God is an option.
At no extra cost, accept Him/Her/It or not.
You're free to believe in *what*ever you want to,
and nobody cares about what is your "what."

Our hymns are de-fanged, no marching armies!
No bleeding martyrs to praise in the words.
We sing a few of the good old-time favorites,
but our book's filled with springtime . . . love . . . even birds.

We don't think it matters much what the words say.
It's the singing together that makes for the fun.
(But it's not all that loose: If a hymn has nine verses,
we religiously suffer to sing every one.)

Holy book? We have none. We honor them all.
Sermons? Whatever! Commandments to rap.
Some teach. Some inspire. Or stimulate thinking.
(Or provide a soft drone for a nice little nap.)

What brings us together? To what do we hold?
Loving thy neighbor's a good place to start.
Add seeking the Truth, wherever that takes us.
Extending the hand . . . and also the heart.

*continued*

Nothing new there, not in what we believe.
The shared common core of values that bind.
But we have no doctrine that spells out just how
they must be pursued and perceived in the mind.

Whatever you are, there's a place for you here
in this friendly and totally welcoming church.
I've been a this . . . and a that . . . and a that.
Now as a Yoo-Hoo,* I've ended my search.

**Unitarian Universalist*

## Animal Adultery

Mr. Porcupine said to Mrs. Porcupine
after Mrs. Porcupine
gave birth to a little baby squirrel,
"Try as you may
and cry as you may
but you can't stick this one on me, old girl."

## Final Passion

The old roué's pulse rate was slowing
while a pretty young nurse was bestowing
a final sweet favor
for a bauble he gave her
when he cried out, "Oh, kiss me, I'm going."

## Southbury*

She sat quietly in the back seat.
And, after a try at talk:
    "You're going to like it there."
        "Yes."
    "You'll have friends to play with."
        "Yes."
    "Your bed, you make your own."
        "Yes."
We settled into silent thought:
    She'll love it there, she will.
        *Will she?*
    Are we deserting her?
        *Yeah, mayb . . . NO!*
    It's the best thing for her.
        *I don't kn . . . YES!*

And then the moment of good-bye:
    "Now you be good, you hear?"
        "Yes."
    "We'll write and come visit you."
        "Yes."
    "And you'll come home, too."
        "Yes."

The school road out and the highway home

took us past the cottage front.
    "There she is. She's waving. Wave."
        "I am."
    "Her hair's so blonde and bright."
        "It's beautiful."
    "She looks . . . she looks sad."
        "I know."

The image of her there in the window pane
made me turn my head
                    away from Jean.
But not before I'd seen
that her head, too, was turned aside
                    away from me.

**school for the mentally challenged.*

## Ball

A bowling ball,
    once rolled,
    will not be told
to haw or hee.

A golfing ball,
    once hit,
    cares not a whit
for golfer's plea.

A basketball,
    once tossed,
    will not be bossed
to score or not.

A football, too,
    once thrown,
    is on its own
to pick its spot.

A volleyball,
    once served,
    will not be curved
to "in" or "out."

A baseball? Yes,
    it, too,
    pays no heed to
what people shout.

In any sport played with ball,
    the most-used crack:
"I wish I had
    that baby back."

## Beauty Done

Do something beautiful.
Not only for the sake
    of beauty done,
but also
and more so
for the sake of what
    doing it
        does for you.

## 5-7-5 Haikus

### Reflections

*Sun on mirrored pond.*
*Shimmering shorelines across.*
*One up and one down.*

### Impatiens

*Wilted impatiens*
*drink the fresh hosed-on water*
*stand and blossom more.*

### Rowing

*Mist on still pond.*
*Bow slices through slick water.*
*Paired puddles eddy.*

### Squirrel

*Squirrel hops along.*
*Body arcs then tail arcs, too.*
*Acorn stops the hops.*

### Speed

*Autumn leaves on pond*
*slide swiftly past the gunwales.*
*Exalting power!*

## Miscellaneous Four-Liners

Prime bad timing is
one pant leg off,
other to your knees
and you have to sneeze.

I'm not a seeker of punishment,
I shun what hurts or makes me sick.
So why does tongue inside my teeth
always follow the Waterpik?

I wonder if the species femme
has really turned so cold,
or is that the species me
has merely grown too old.

If I could see myself as others see me,
I suspect that I would change a thing or two.
But if I *could* see me as others see me,
do you suppose they'd see me as they do?

When I garden, my wife listens closely,
not waiting to spot a mistake.
She just knows that sooner or later
she will hear me step on a rake.

*continued*

Take an xmas office party
and all you need to queer it
is one romantic smarty
with too much sexmas spirit.

## Both Sides

*News item: President George W. Bush says*
*we should teach both sides.*

"You know what those evolution people say?"
    the Intelligent Designist asked.
"They say that us human beings
    just happened bit by bit
                by *accident*!
    Because some worms kinda felt
    they needed arms and legs,
                and heads and brains
                as good as ours.
That to survive, they had to be
            just like you and me!"

*"Well," the Evolutionist sighed,*
*"I don't know where to start.*
*But, for just one thing,*

*the lower form of life*
*does not decide how it should evolve*
*from what it was.*
*It just does."*

"Just like that, huh?" the ID preacher smirked.
"Well, we've got scientists who say
that something as complicated
as an eye
or an ear
or opposing thumb
could not just accidentally become.

But never mind all that.
The key thing is
we've got two sides here.
We've got us a debate!
Fair's fair.
Just listen to the man
who took the Presidential oath:
'Got to teach both!'"

## Hot Air on a Hot Day

At the county fair, the candidates orated
six hours
full steam and unabated.
And when they finally ended,
Old Seth, who doesn't hear too well,
asked his brother, Jonathan, to tell
him what the candidates had said all day.
And Jonathan cupped his hands to yell,
*"They didn't say!"*

## Not Yet

Whittlin' on the porch,
Vernon stopped his knife
in mid-cut
when the tourist
asked about his life:
"You've lived it *all* in this one house, I bet!"

Turnin' in the blade,
then tappin' on his lip
with jackknife,
how you do in thought
with fingertip,
Vern gave it time and then replied, "Not yet!"

Ezra, drinkin' beer
the time he told about it, nearly choked
from laughin'.
Cy coughed a red-faced fit
right through the pipe he smoked.
And Ben (he's ninety-six), his pants got wet.

## Report from the Other Side of Ninety

What is it like to live on really old?
I mean well past the average for men.
I guess that it varies
from codger to codger,
but probably some things
apply to us all.

Take the libido, what happens to that?
For better or worse, it stays pretty strong.
Only once it was centered
in the region "down there."
And now it's restricted
to "from the neck up."

What comes as a shock (a downer as well)
is finding one day while working outside
that you can't lift the Sakrete.
And, when golfing, your drive
leaves your ball where it's always
the one that's "back there."

You have to accept (you don't have a choice)
a number of things you can no longer do.
Take that flow you once arced
in a strong golden stream.

That's a memory now
as you stand in close.

Once in the bathing room mirror you struck
poses that brought on superior smirks.
But now for the underside muscles
that hang a bit limply
and jiggle when patted,
a grin of chagrin.

Then there are *new* things you have to accept.
Your own and unique set of aches and of pains.
And "conditions" you now have
that bring into your life
the pillbox that tells you
the day of the week.

You're calmer more days . . . accepting of things.
So many, you've learned, are not worth the stress.
And also with old age
you are given the right
to ignore what annoys.
To not give a damn!

That includes the shuffling off of this coil.
You're in the bonus years now anyway.
(Though to have that disinterest
you've got to feel certain

*continued*

that nothing can touch you
once you have escaped.)

Oh . . . MEMORY . . . I almost forgot it.
Yes, some of us tragically lose it.
But, thankfully, most of us
hold on to what's vital:
retaining our contact
with those who we love.

## By Love Controlled

*News item: Vatican says US should not provide birth control devices to third-world countries.*

The prelates say
  we must not tell
  of love except *au naturel.*
Poor Countries
  must not base their tactics
  upon US prophylactics.
Nor should we let foreign aid
  dictate how foreign wives are laid.

All this
  is not to say that priests
  want third-world poor
  to swell like yeast.
Oh no!
  These worldly celibates
  know how to cheat the amorous fates.
Their plan is sanctified
              and plain.
"Make love with rhythm
              or abstain!"

And on this self-control they base
  survival of the human face.

*continued*

And so they will
   until the day
   (that isn't very far away)
the day
   on which there will not be
   the room for more humanity.

When universal birth control
   will be imposed by love's own toll.
With neither place nor room
   for one defection.
   None for even one erection.
   None for horizontal passion,
   nor for love in any fashion.

Then future hordes will have to
                        stand and die
                        nose to nose,
                        toe to toe,
                        eye to eye.

## Idiot Selling

It's gonna go down.
        It's gonna go down.
                It's gonna go down.
Gotta sell.
Gotta sell.
Gotta sell.
And so I sold.
        And so I sold.
                And so I sold.
And whad'ya know,
the Dow went down.

Told you so!

## Regret

There's something I regret
　　most every day:
all the should-have-saids
　　I didn't say.
I don't mean only
　　loving things.
Don't mark me down as soft.
I mean those words
　　I should have said
to tell those bastards off.

## Epitaph

All my life I have conformed.
 Man and boy.
By the rules I have performed.
 Pride and joy.

Earning the approving pat
 on my head.
"You are good." I wanted that
 to be said.

What will my notation be
 in the log
of my life? Well, I can see,
 "*Good* dog."

CPSIA information can be obtained at www.ICGtesting.com
Printed in the USA
BVOW08s0424220515

401277BV00001B/1/P